THAT'S A GOOD QUESTION, CANADA!

Edited by Ty Reynolds

Script:

the writers' group

Calgary, Alberta, Canada

Published by Script: the writers' group inc.
Copyright © 1990 by the Canadian Broadcasting Corporation

Cover design by Ty Reynolds

Individual questions and answers in this book were first broadcast by CBC Radio stations across Canada and are used with permission.

Manufactured in Canada

10 9 8 7 6 5 4 3 2 1

Canadian Cataloguing in Publication Data

Main entry under title:

That's a good question, Canada!

Canadian ed.
ISBN 0-9694287-2-3

1. Questions and answers.   2. Radio broadcasting -- Canada
-- Miscellanea.   I. Reynolds, Ty, 1956-

AG195.T44 1990   031.02   C90-090554-9

Where did these questions and answers come from?

The questions in this book were spawned by the enquiring minds of CBC listeners from coast to coast. Radio shows that contributed questions are

Daybreak (Kelowna)
The Calgary Eyeopener (Calgary)
Edmonton AM (Edmonton)
The Morning Edition (Regina)
Great Northwest (Thunder Bay)
Morning North (Sudbury)
Information Morning (Moncton)
Island Morning (Charlottetown)
Information Morning (Halifax)

The answers to the questions in this book represent the research of many people who work for CBC Radio across Canada. CBC staff were helped out by hundreds of individuals and organizations who provided the information and expertise necessary to answer these Good Questions. To both these groups of people, we offer our appreciation.

Particular thanks are extended to regular information supply lines at federal, provincial, and municipal government departments and agencies.

Who made this book possible?

A portion of the purchase price of this book is being donated to local charities. The charities receiving proceeds are

   in B.C. - the local Canadian Red Cross Society
   in Alberta - local Food Banks
   in Saskatchewan - the local Canadian Red Cross
    Society
   in N.E. Ontario - the Thunder Bay Native Satellite
    Centre
   in N.W. Ontario - the local Canadian Red Cross
    Society
   in New Brunswick - the Mapleton Food Bank
   in P.E.I. - the United Way of P.E.I.
   in Nova Scotia - the Halifax Metro Food Bank

The donation of proceeds to charity is only possible due to the contributions of time, supplies, and services by the businesses involved in the production and distribution of this book. We would like to thank

   Canadian Air Cargo, Canadian Airlines
    International,
   Script: the writers' group inc.,
   Greyhound Courier Express,
   Acadian Bus Lines,
   GTO Printing,
   and
   United Graphic Services

for their kindness and generosity.

Introduction

In the fall of next year, I'll mark my twentieth anniversary of hosting CBC morning radio (though I have taken a few years off between then and now). In those years, I've learned a few things about radio. The three most profound are:

1. Unlike television (where I was for most of those missing years) radio is an individual medium. People listen to it by themselves — in the car, in the kitchen, in bed or when they should be doing their homework.

2: It's Sydney, Nova Scotia, and Sidney (with an i), B.C. Unless, of course, it's the other way around. (It's also Ernest Seton Thompson and not Ernest Thompson Seton — isn't it?)

3: and the one I'm really sure of: The listeners are all smarter than I am.

I learned this early on, when I received my first letter correcting a fact, if you can believe such a thing. That was maybe nineteen years and three weeks ago next fall. (It took a few days for the mail to arrive.) Since then, I've learned it again, about once a day. If I had any doubts, I'd have erased them when I saw the first edition of That's a Good Question!

Good answers, as anyone knows, are relatively easy. Good *questions* are the hard things to come up with. And whoever it was at The Calgary Eyeopener — I think it was Val Boser, but since she later worked for Morningside, I may be prejudiced — who first suggested getting listeners to pose questions, which is where these books began, is a genius.

Now stations from Cape Breton to Prince Rupert have picked up on the idea. A lot of funds have been raised for good purposes and a lot of fascinating facts have been dug up and published — all because the listeners, whose questions these are, were smart. There is *tons* of good stuff in here.

If this is such a good idea, in fact — and it is — you probably wonder why Morningside hasn't stolen it.

Good question.

Peter Gzowski,
Morningside
October 1990

Table of Contents

Who is the Murphy of Murphy's Law?

There are several theories that claim to identify Murphy. While none can be proven, they all seem to support his dictum, "If anything can go wrong, it will."

One theory states that there never was a Murphy; the name is merely a representation of the common man against whom the world conspires. Cartoonist Al Capp captured this essence of Murphy in his comic strip, L'il Abner, with the character Joe Btfsplk, the hapless little loser under a perpetual rain cloud.

Another theory says that Murphy was a school teacher. During a math class, Murphy was trying to demonstrate the laws of probability to his students. He told them each to spread peanut butter on a slice of bread. The students then threw the bread in the air to find out how many slices would land peanut butter-side up. The experiment was not completed, however, as all the data could not be collected. Twenty-eight slices landed on the floor; one stuck to the ceiling. Murphy's law of data collection was born: whenever a peanut butter sandwich can stick to the ceiling, it will.

The Los Angeles Times claims to have found the most likely answer. According to the paper, there was a development engineer named Captain Ed Murphy working at Edwards Airforce Base in 1949. No matter what he tried, Murphy could not get the project he was working on to work properly. Murphy became so frustrated by the constant mistakes made by his technician that he complained to a colleague "if there's any way to do it wrong, he'll find it."

The story is not part of official US Airforce history, but we do know there was an Ed Murphy who graduated from West Point. He was a pilot and engineer, and he worked on a number of post-war research projects.

Then again, another law attributed to Murphy, whoever he was, says that, on the rare occasion when something is popular and successful, the wrong person will get the credit.

Why do babies smell different than adults?

The smell of a human being is caused mainly by sweat. Babies and adults both sweat, but baby sweat is purer.

Sweat glands do not fully develop until puberty. When mature, the sweat glands produce steroids that are secreted in the sweat. When these steroids in sweat combine with bacteria naturally occurring on the body, a strong odour is created. The bacteria break down the steroids, and the chemical reaction produces an odour.

The bacteria on a baby's body do not produce the same odour because the baby's sweat does not contain the steroids found in adult sweat.

Why is there no channel 1 on TV sets?

Television broadcasting technology has been around since the 1920s. During the 1930s, the CBS and NBC radio networks were experimenting with television. In 1939, the first commercial programs in North America were broadcast to the hundred or so privately-owned television sets in New York City. But growth of the fledgling medium was halted abruptly by the Second World War.

The early television sets were able to receive only a limited number of broadcast frequencies. Unlike radio, which uses the actual multi-digit frequency number to identify broadcasting stations, television assigns a simpler code number to each receivable frequency: channel one, channel two, channel three, etc.

During the war, military requirements changed the course of communications research and development. The war put plans for an entertainment-based television industry on hold. By the time the networks were again ready to launch television programming in 1948, the military had established its claim on the channel one frequency for two-way radio communications. Rather than realign the channel numbers and the remaining frequencies, manufacturers simply designed their sets to begin with channel two.

Modern television sets are specifically designed with internal operating circuits so that they are unable to receive channel one.

Which trees produce the most oxygen?

Trees, and most other plants, release oxygen as a by-product of photosynthesis. Plants containing chlorophyll absorb water, carbon dioxide, and energy from the sun to produce organic compounds; oxygen is released into the air as a by-product. Photosynthesis in trees takes place in the leaves; chlorophyll is the green substance that gives the leaves their colour. The amount of oxygen produced by a single tree depends on a number of factors, including leaf size, climate and weather, soil density, water supply, air quality, and health of the tree.

Tree species with broad leaves release more oxygen than smaller-leafed species. The greater surface area exposes more leaf cells to the atmosphere and to sunlight.

Trees of a given species generally grow faster in a moderate climate than in a harsher environment. With a higher metabolism, rapidly-growing trees process water and carbon dioxide at a faster rate, producing more oxygen.

City trees produce up to 15 times more oxygen than their country cousins. That's because of the much higher carbon dioxide content of city air due to industry and especially automobile emissions. Urban planners are becoming increasingly aware of the environmental, as well as the aesthetic, contribution trees make to city life. Trees nearing the end of their life cycles are being replaced, and as trees are planted in new neighborhoods, planners are taking into consideration each species' capacity to produce oxygen and filter the air of pollutants. Some of the best trees for this purpose are poplars, American elm, green ash, bur oak, and Strathmore flowering crabapple trees.

Why do birds face the same direction when perched on a high-tension wire?

Hydro lines and telephone wires make excellent high-vantage points for birds such as starlings and blackbirds. From such locations, the birds are able to survey the area for food. But they are also exposed and vulnerable to attack.

When a flock of birds sits along a wire, most face the same way. However, one or two usually sit facing the opposite direction, acting as lookouts, covering the rear. These birds are exposed to the greatest danger. If a predator such as a hawk is spotted by the lookouts, the members of the flock are able to take off as a group and stay together. The individuals facing the opposite direction must take off and turn around to catch up.

As the predator comes closer, the flock gathers in a tighter formation. The tight formation is an effort to scare away the predator. If this effort is successful, the predator will turn its attention to stragglers, which pose no threat and are easier to catch.

How can Crimestoppers pay for information if the informant remains anonymous?

Crimestoppers is a program that teams up local police and media; with the cooperation of the media, attention is focused on a specific unsolved criminal incident. In an effort to gather evidence from readers, listeners, and viewers, newspapers and radio stations release details about the case, and TV stations show re-enactments of the offence. As an incentive, cash rewards are offered for information leading to an arrest.

The program and the rewards are financed entirely by donations from individuals and corporations. It is not run by police, nor supported by tax dollars. Newspaper space and broadcasting time are either donated by the respective medium or underwritten by donors.

Crimestoppers began in Albuquerque, New Mexico in the late 1970s. In 1982, Calgary became the first city in Canada to try the program. It has since been adopted by most major centres in Canada (except in the province of Quebec), and in the United States. There are also many Rural Crimestoppers programs across the continent.

A tipster's call to Crimestoppers is not recorded, and the caller remains anonymous. No personal information is required, and callers can be identified only by a number that is assigned to them when they place the call. When the information is passed on, the police are not even told it was received from a Crimestoppers' call, since that, depending on the case, may help reveal the source. For the same reason, many Crimestoppers' successes are not publicized as such. Informants never have to appear in court because the police cannot subpoena someone if they don't know who they are.

Callers who provide information are advised of when to call back to find out if there are any developments in the case and if they are therefore eligible for the reward. The cash award must be picked up in person. The claimant does not have to be the person who called, but he or she must give the identification number and may be asked about the nature of the information provided.

It should be obvious, then, that an informant's representative must be trustworthy. Since the caller remains unidentified, claims of false representation cannot be proven.

What makes the rattle in a rattlesnake's tail?

A rattlesnake's rattle is made from remnants of shed skin. All snakes shed their skin as they grow. The shedding begins at the head, and the skin peels back whole like a pair of socks.

Instead of peeling the skin away completely like most other snakes, however, the rattlesnake keeps a dried-up button of skin on its tail. As each layer of skin peels away, another button is added, forming a loosely-connected, interlocking series. When the rattlesnake is threatened, it vibrates its tail in an effort to scare away its enemies. The buttons bang against each other, making the rattling sound.

How does a spider get its first line across?

After a spider finds an appropriate spot to call home, it begins construction of a new web. It first climbs to the highest spot to be webbed and lets out the first silk line. The end of this line is sticky and is anchored in place. The spider releases more silk, then jumps from its perch, dangling from its line. As it swings from side to side, the spider releases more silk until an appropriate second spot is reached. If weather permits, the spider may instead let a length of silk dangle in the breeze until the sticky, free end adheres to a solid object. The line is then glued in place and cut by the spider.

Once the first line is in place, construction of the main web begins. The spokes of the web, made of non-sticky silk, are spun first. The sticky silk that spirals around the spokes is then laid down. The spider is not immune to its own sticky web — it must stay on the non-sticky silk spokes as it moves around on the web. A spider may become trapped in its own web during a strong wind, or when a much larger animal walks or flies through it.

Spider silk is very strong — stronger than steel of equal fineness. It is also very elastic, able to stretch and contract without breaking as the temperature and humidity change. Because of these properties, spider silk is used by manufacturers of such optical instruments as gun sights.

Getting silk from a captive spider for such purposes is called silking. To silk a spider, the silker carefully mounts the spider to a cork board. The silker then tickles the spider's abdomen with a camel's hair brush to stimulate silk production. The silk is wound onto special spools designed to prevent the strand from touching itself.

Species of spiders used in commercial silk production include the Golden Silk Spider and the Black Widow.

Why do parts of our bodies fall asleep?

The lack of feeling in our limbs that we call "sleep" is the result of restricted blood circulation. This occurs when pressure is applied to a limb for a long enough period of time that nerve cells of the limb are deprived of oxygen, thereby limiting communication between the limb and the brain.

For example, if you sit with your left leg over your right leg, trying to stay awake through the entire duration of your neighbour's home movies, your right leg will fall asleep. When you finally stand up, your right leg will collapse because the brain has temporarily lost control of the leg muscles.

In most cases, circulation is restricted for only a short time, and feeling quickly returns as the blood pressure in the limb returns to normal. We feel a tingling sensation as the nerves "wake up." However, in extreme cases where circulation has been restricted for days, there may be permanent nerve damage.

Why do hubcaps and propellers appear to spin backwards on TV?

Stagecoach spokes, airplane propellers, helicopter rotor blades, and the wheels of the Beverly Hillbillies' jalopy all appear to spin backwards on TV and in the movies because of an optical illusion.

Film and video both produce the illusion of movement by flashing a series of still images on a screen so fast that the brain cannot process the images individually. Instead, the images are blurred together and appear to be moving. A child's flip book works the same way — as the pages are quickly flipped, the individual drawings appear to be one moving image.

Film images are projected at 24 frames per second. If a wheel spinning at exactly 24 revolutions per second is filmed, it would appear motionless on the screen, since each frame would look the same. Whether the wheel appears to be spinning forward or backward depends on its position as each frame is shot.

For example, let's say one of the spokes of a wheel spinning clockwise is in the one o'clock position in the first frame. Regardless of how many times it may have rotated clockwise between frames, if the spoke is in the twelve o'clock position in the next frame, and in the eleven o'clock position in the next, and so on, the wheel will appear to be spinning counterclockwise when the film is projected. If the spoke is at one o'clock, then two o'clock, then three o'clock, and so on, the wheel will appear to be spinning clockwise.

This phenomenon is most pronounced when the spinning object is changing speeds. When a fighter pilot comes in for a landing, for example, his propeller appears to be spinning in one direction, then the other, before the plane comes to a full stop.

Do lobsters really scream when they're boiled, and why do they turn red when they're cooked?

If you were sitting in a vat of boiling water, you'd scream and turn red, too. But in the lobster's case, there is no scream, and there is a chemical reason for the change in colour.

Noises *are* produced as a lobster is boiled alive, but the sounds are not voices. As the lobster's body heats up in the shell, pockets of air in the cavities and joints expand. If enough pressure builds inside the body, the air will make whistle-like sounds as it escapes through small openings in the shell.

As for the colour shift, a lobster's shell contains red pigment molecules that combine with a protein to create the camouflaging colours of the lobster. Live lobsters are usually blue-green or brown with flecks of yellow. When the lobster is boiled, the protein is denatured, or deformed, by the heat. The pigment remains, however, turning the shell red.

Why are TV commercials louder than the regular programs?

Television stations frequently receive audience complaints accusing them of deliberately boosting the volume during commercial breaks. But the commercials are not treated any differently by the broadcasters than the programs, and they are not any louder. The recording meters of a tape recorder hooked up to a television would reveal that a commercial does not "peak" at a higher level. This can also be seen on the newer video cassette recorders that have built-in audio meters.

The broadcasting and recording industries use a continuous alignment tone as a standard audio level. This tone is the sound that a station broadcasts along with the test pattern or colour bars when it is not on the air. The advertising agencies that produce television commercials use the same tone to establish a recording's audio level. The tone at the beginning of each commercial the station broadcasts is matched with the continuous alignment tone so that all programming is broadcast at the same level.

However, air time is very expensive, and commercial producers have very little time in which to get their message across to the viewers. There are several techniques they use to make their commercials stand out and seem louder. Continuous sound seems louder than sound that rises and falls. Commercials therefore often contain a continuous assault of music and talk. The commercials that seem most persistent often employ fast talkers since the words seem louder when they are compressed.

Whether or not a commercial seems to be an

assault to one's senses also depends on how welcome the noise is. During a televised hockey game, for example, viewers rarely object to the combination of music, crowd noise, commentators' talk, and the sounds of the game itself, even though the noise is constant.

Viewers have complained about loud commercials since the early days of television, but sales figures indicate that commercials that seem loud are effective.

Why are pairs of long underwear called longjohns?

According to Stanfield's, Canada's leading underwear manufacturer, the name "longjohns" comes to us from the world of boxing. In the early days of boxing as a professional sport, one popular boxer was John L. Sullivan. In 1880, Sullivan entered the record books as the last bareknuckled Champion of the World. Sullivan always wore long underwear-like pants during his fights.

Other boxers of the period also wore the long pants into the ring, but because of his stature, Sullivan's name was attached to them. They became John L's or Long John's, and eventually, longjohns.

How does Silly Putty work?

Silly Putty is the children's toy that bounces like a ball, breaks when jerked apart, and stretches when pulled. Silly Putty was first marketed as a toy in 1949, after several years in development as a substitute for rubber.

During the Second World War, General Electric's silicone division was conducting experiments to produce a synthetic rubber. During one such series of tests, an engineer mixed boric acid with silicone oil. When he poured out the mixture, it bounced on the floor. The pliant substance stretched more than soft rubber, rebounded more than hard rubber, and did not disintegrate in extreme conditions. But the substance made a poor substitute for rubber because it behaved like a liquid. Once moulded, it slowly lost its shape and oozed into a puddle. This is why Silly Putty should always be returned to its plastic eggshell for storage.

In an effort to find a useful purpose for the curiosity, General Electric mailed samples to engineers around the world in 1945. But it took a true genius to put the putty to use. A toy store owner and former advertising copy-writer from New Haven, Connecticut, noticed at a demonstration how the substance, unofficially called nutty putty, kept adults amused for hours.

He bought a large wad of the nutty putty, hired a student from Yale to fill brightly-coloured plastic eggshells with one-ounce portions, and sold the putty as a toy in his store. That year, Silly Putty outsold everything else on the shelves. The product was immediately mass-marketed, earning about six million dollars annually through the 1950s and '60s.

The molecules of Silly Putty have a lattice structure. If the putty is pulled apart slowly, the criss-cross of molecules stretches like an accordion. If the putty is suddenly jerked apart, the interlocking molecules break apart with a snapping sound. When it is rolled into a ball and dropped, the sudden force of the impact pushes the lattice in on itself. The lattice quickly springs back into shape, however, causing the ball to rebound.

Why is Scotch Tape called Scotch Tape?

According to legend at 3M, the company that manufactures Scotch Tape, the name comes from an incident in the 1920s. According to the story, a customer was using masking tape for a paint job, but the tape wouldn't stick to the surface of what he was painting. The customer complained, telling the salesman to tell his "Scotch" boss to put more adhesive on the tape.

In those days, to be called Scotch was to be accused of being cheap. However the epithet was intended, William McKnight, the owner of 3M and himself a Scot, took the customer's advice and produced a new, stickier tape, which he called Scotch Tape.

How much money do Canadians spend on lottery tickets, and how are the proceeds spent?

There are five different corporations, divided along regional lines, running the lotteries in Canada. They all follow the same guidelines, which determine how the money received from ticket sales is distributed. According to the guidelines, the largest portion, about 46 per cent, should go toward prizes, while 38 per cent should go to the provinces and territories for various athletic, cultural, and social endeavors.

The remaining funds cover the overhead costs of the lotteries. Eight per cent goes to operating expenses, six per cent is paid to retailers as commissions, and two per cent covers the cost of printing tickets.

The lottery business has been steadily growing since its introduction. For example, during the Western Canada Lottery Corporation's first year in 1973-74, western Canadians spent $22 million on tickets. In 1988, the figure was $502 million. Across the country, Canadians gamble over $18 million *per week* on the lotteries. About half that amount is spent on Lotto 6/49 tickets.

Why do Canadians say "zed" and Americans say "zee"?

The letter Z comes from the French, who took it from the Greek letter zeta. The French abbreviated the pronunciation to "zed," which was later adopted by the English. But in some areas of Britain, such as Suffolk and Norfolk, the pronunciation was further abbreviated to "zee". This local variation was not considered to be proper Oxford English.

The 17th century settlers of the New England states were mainly from the "zee" speaking parts of Britain. When the American nationalist Daniel Webster began work on his dictionary, his goal was to ensure that the American language was distinct from that of Great Britain. In 1828, he recognized "zee" as the official pronunciation of Z. It is also because of his dictionary that many words have different British and American spellings.

Meanwhile, many of the English settlers in Canada were Scots and Scots-Irish. They used the "zed" pronunciation. "Zed" was formally accepted by Canada in the early 20th century when the government, to display loyalty to the crown, officially recognized British pronunciations and spellings.

But for all the differences, in the end it hardly matters. As Fred Astaire sang to Ginger Rogers, "You say po-tay-toes, I say po-tah-toes. Let's call the whole thing off."

Why doesn't Mickey Mouse have a tail anymore?

The Walt Disney Studio's first release was the animated short, *Steamboat Willie*, in 1928. It virtually assured the fledgling company's success for two reasons: it was the first animated cartoon to use synchronized sound, and it introduced Mickey Mouse to the world.

Since then, the world's most famous mouse has gone through a number of transformations. In the 1940 feature film *Fantasia*, he was given pupils to make his face more expressive. Prior to *Fantasia*, his eyes were merely black discs. Briefly, during the 1940s, Mickey had three-dimensional ears, but they were dropped in favour of the original ears, perfectly round no matter from what angle they are seen.

Mickey's tail was on and off between 1928 and 1953. For the studio artists, drawing in the tail and animating it so it moved naturally was time-consuming without contributing much to the project. To avoid drawing the tail, the animators gave the character a pair of pants that, besides being the decent thing to do, gave Mickey a place to tuck in his tail. The tail has simply been forgotten about since 1953.

Mickey Mouse dolls and toys do not have a tail for a more practical reason. It would be too easy for a long thin tail to break off and present a danger to small children tempted to swallow it.

Why is paper a standard 8-1/2"x11" or 8-1/2"x14" size?

Until the early 1920s, paper came in several sizes, depending on national conventions. At this time, an international committee was formed to standardize paper for legal and diplomatic purposes.

At the time, the British were using 8"x10", other European countries were using 9"x12", and the Americans were using 8"x10-1/2" paper. The committee decided to split the difference, and settled on 8-1/2"x11" for letters, 8-1/2"x13" for foolscap, and 8-1/2"x14" for legal stationery.

The American government did not accept the recommendations of the committee, and continued to use 8"x10-1/2". But this size created problems for the government when Xerox introduced its photocopiers. The machines would only accept 8-1/2"x11" and 8-1/2"x13", so the government changed its policy in the face of technology. However, Xerox did modify its copiers to accommodate the legal-sized stationery. Today, most photocopier manufacturers produce machines able to accommodate any size paper up to 11"x17".

In 1973, the Canadian General Standard Board settled on 8-1/2"x11" sized paper for letters, and 8-1/2"x14" paper for legal documents.

When was the first grain elevator built in Canada?

The grain elevator is as much a symbol of the prairies as the Eiffel Tower is of France. However, the first grain elevator in North America was not constructed in the prairies, but rather in the industrial heartland; it was built in Buffalo, New York, in 1842. Canada's first grain elevator was built in 1879, in Niverville, Manitoba. The round wooden bin, designed by William Hespeler and John Wittick, had a capacity of about 90 tons. The capacity of modern grain elevators ranges from 2,000 tons to 50,000 tons.

The Ogilvie Milling Company built the first rectangular Canadian grain elevator in 1881 at Gretna, Manitoba. The design was copied from elevators in North and South Dakota and in Minnesota. The rectangular style, familiar to all those who have travelled through the small towns of the prairies, was adopted because it was easier than the circular style to build.

Why are British physicians addressed as Doctor and British surgeons as Mister?

Until the final days of the Roman Empire, monks and barbers both engaged in surgery. In 1123, the Pope announced that monks should not shed blood. Monks continued to practice medicine, but the fields of surgery and dentistry were left exclusively to the barbers.

In the 1300s, some apprentice barbers began specializing in surgery, often becoming more skilled than their teachers. These barbers became known as pure surgeons. But the pure surgeons could not be addressed as Doctor because they apprenticed, did not have a university education, and did not speak Latin.

Henry VIII introduced an act of Parliament in 1540 that re-united the surgeon-barbers and the pure surgeons, calling them Masters and Governors of the Mystery and Commonality of Barbery and Surgery. As a result, any practitioner had the right to be addressed as Master, which has since been corrupted to Mister. George II broke up the union in 1745, but to this day in Britain, male members of the Royal College of Surgeons are addressed as Mister. Female members are addressed as Miss or Mrs.

What is the origin of the necktie?

Men have been wearing some form of cloth around their necks since ancient times, but the modern necktie dates back to the 17th century. The fashion was born after a group of Croatian mercenaries had come to France. The French admired how the Croats knotted their linen scarves around their necks, and adopted the look. The French called the neckwear *cravates*, from the French word for Croat.

A popular sport in Britain at the time was called "driving the four-in-hand". Members of each team, driving carriages led by four horses, identified themselves with a neck cloth similar to the French version. The knot the British sportsmen used is now known as the four-in-hand. And since then, ties have been decorated with regimental and school colours, which are still proudly worn by members of the British Establishment.

Beau Brummel, the British arbiter of men's fashion in the early 1800s, made further refinements. Brummel, friend of the Prince Regent, sparked a fad for turned-down collars. He then had the neck cloth pressed and starched, and wore it underneath the collar, creating the necktie we recognize today. Brummel's variety of ties and the many ways he tied them created a sensation. How to tie the perfect knot became the sartorial world's Holy Grail.

Since then, ties have been the focus of men's fashion and subjected to much analysis. The tie has become a symbol for anything from masculine virility to corporate conformity.

Bow ties also come from the neck scarf. The first ones were six inches wide, but the ties have since been modified to have smaller bows, an additional lining, and every young boy's friend, a metal clip-on.

What causes the dark circles around our eyes when we're tired?

While the human body sleeps, waste products are collected from cells for eventual elimination. If we stay up longer than usual or don't get enough sleep, the waste isn't collected, and it accumulates in the spaces in the body between the cells, including the loose tissue around the eyes.

But one's beauty rest is not enough to totally eliminate the dark circles, since this effect is also caused by shadows around the eyes. This is most noticeable if a strong light source is overhead. Portrait photographers often light their subjects with a soft side light or use a reflector from below to reduce shadows on the face.

As a person ages, the shadow becomes more pronounced because the tissue around, and especially below, the eye loses its elasticity and starts to sag. Baggy eyelids cast an even deeper shadow, making the dark circles more pronounced.

Who designs our money?

The designs on the front and back of Canadian paper currency and coins are designed by artists working in the graphic and engraving industries. The work is commissioned by the Bank of Canada and is subject to the approval of the federal Minister of Finance.

When a new design is being considered, the Bank of Canada's concerns are not limited merely to the aesthetic. The bank confers with its printers and international security consultants to reduce the possibility that the new money can be counterfeited. The Governor of the Bank of Canada then passes the recommendations on to the Minister of Finance for approval.

Although the United States rarely changes the design of its money, Canada and many European countries make significant alterations about every 15 years to reduce the risk of counterfeiting. The new, simpler design of Canadian currency is intended to make counterfeiting errors more apparent.

The most recent changes on Canadian bills, from panoramic scenes to simpler designs on the back, and to larger portraits and numerals on the front, were incorporated as an aid to the visually impaired. The new look also makes the bills machine-readable and makes it easier for change machines to tell different denominations apart.

How do police radar units work?

The police radar unit used for nabbing speeders is based on the Doppler Effect. The device transmits a microwave beam set at a certain frequency. When the beam bounces off a vehicle, the frequency is changed by the speed of the car. The change in frequency is directly proportional to the speed of the car. The radar unit compares the frequencies of the outgoing and incoming beams to determine the car's speed.

The radar units used by police are accurate to within one half of a kilometer per hour. They are also tested several times a day with a tuning fork for accuracy, which ensures that the emitted beam is calibrated to the correct frequency.

However, this does not mean the system is flawless. Speeding tickets based on radar readings have been successfully challenged in court. The beam transmitted by the radar gun travels in an arc eight degrees wide. The width of the beam is therefore 15 per cent of the distance of the radar unit from the target. If the target is 1,000 feet away, the beam is 150 feet wide. A beam that wide can land on more than one vehicle at a time, so the police officer must decide which vehicle is moving faster.

Another problem arises when the radar gun is aimed at a flat surface. Some flat surfaces, like the roof of a car, act like mirrors, reflecting the radar beam. The officer may be aiming at one vehicle, but be getting a reading from the vehicle behind it.

What is the magazine with the largest circulation?

The magazine with the largest circulation and greatest number of editions world-wide is actually a combination of several magazines: Reader's Digest.

In 1920, DeWitt Wallace of St. Paul, Minnesota, saw a need for a small publication that would contain the most noteworthy articles from the many magazines available. He felt that readers did not have the time or money to keep up with the myriad of magazines, but still wanted to be well-informed. Wallace was unable to secure the interest of a publisher or other backers, so he and his wife formed the Reader's Digest Association in 1921, which began publishing in 1922.

The digest was an immediate success. At first, other magazines were willing to grant reprint rights without fees, viewing the added readership as free publicity. But as Reader's Digest grew, it came to be seen as competition. From 1933 to the 1950s, Wallace engaged in the controversial practice of commissioning articles for other magazines. The articles were then reprinted in Reader's Digest. Smaller publications welcomed the free copy, but others were critical, charging that Wallace was interfering with the content of too many magazines through his "planted" stories, which often reflected his own views.

Reader's Digest is currently published in 15 languages: English, Spanish, Portuguese, Chinese, Swedish, Finnish, Norwegian, Danish, French, German, Dutch, Italian, Korean, Arabic, and Hindi. In English, there are Canadian, American, British, Australian, South African, New Zealand, Indian, and

Asian editions. It is also available in large print for the sight impaired, in Braille for the blind, and as a talking record edition. Worldwide, Reader's Digest has a circulation of over 28 million.

Why are share values on the stock market stated in fractions of dollars, and why is market activity recorded in points?

Stock market share values were originally stated in multiples of whole dollars, but as shares were divided and resold, those values also had to be divided.

The decimal system works when a dollar is split in half, then is split in half again to create a quarter. With further splits, however, the decimal system becomes clumsy. Instead, the dollar value of shares is recorded using fractions. Share prices are divided into 1/2, 1/4, and 1/8. Some American markets further divide the dollar into 1/16 and 1/32.

The point system is used to monitor trends in stock prices. In the case of the Toronto Stock Exchange (TSE), the values of the top 300 blue-chip stocks were used as a guide to peg the market at 1000 points in January 1977. The daily TSE average indicates the relative value of these stocks compared to 1977.

What is aspirin and how does it work?

Aspirin, or acetylsalicylic acid, is the man-made version of a powder derived from the bark of the willow tree. The powder has been used since ancient times as a medicine to relieve fever, toothache, gout, and other maladies. Aspirin is now the most widely used self-administered drug in the world.

Charles Frederick von Gerhardt, a chemist from the French province of Alsace, first synthesized aspirin in 1853. However, he concluded that the drug was no more effective than salicin, the extract from the willow bark. It was not until 1893 that German chemist Felix Hoffman, employed at the Farbenfabriken Bayer drug company, did more tests. Hoffman was so desperate to relieve his father's arthritis that he prepared a batch of the substance he had read about. His tests were much more successful than von Gerhardt's.

The Bayer company was quick to capitalize on Hoffman's discovery. The word *aspirin* comes from *Spiraea ulmaria*, the Latin name of the meadowsweet plant used in aspirin production. Aspirin was first marketed as a loose powder, and Bayer introduced the tablet form in 1915.

The German company was forced to give up the trademark name Aspirin as part of the war reparations after World War I. When the Treaty of Versailles was signed in 1919, the name was surrendered to England, France, the United States, and Russia. After several years of corporate warring, the famed American judge Learned Hand ruled that the word had slipped into common use and that no company could claim ownership or collect royalties.

For a drug with such wide acceptance, very little is known of how aspirin works. Some scientists believe it does not relieve symptoms, but rather raises the body's threshold of pain. Others claim it alters the body's chemistry. Aspirin is known to aggravate stomach ulcers, but is otherwise considered to be a safe treatment for a wide variety of ills and is perhaps the closest thing to a legitimate wonder drug. Current medical research is exploring the use of aspirin in heart attack and stroke prevention.

Why is New York called The Big Apple?

According to the New York Convention and Visitors' Bureau, the city got its nickname in the 1920s from travelling sportsmen and entertainers. To these people who made their living touring, there were a lot of apples in the barrel, but New York was the biggest of them all. Or as Ol' Blue Eyes put it, "If I can make it there, I'll make it anywhere; it's up to you, New York, New York."

The Bureau officially adopted the Big Apple name in 1971 and now includes it in all of its promotions. This isn't the first epithet for the city, however; New York has also been called Fun City, Gotham, The Naked City, The City That Never Sleeps, and The City So Nice They Named It Twice. But then again, so is Walla Walla, Washington.

How do seedless fruit trees reproduce?

Trees and vines that produce seedless fruit, such as mandarin oranges and grapes, are genetic aberrations of nature. Their fruit is sterile, unable to reproduce more seedless trees and vines, and so such trees are highly prized when found.

Once a seedless tree is discovered, its branches are grafted onto normal trees. The fruit will continue to be seedless, and production will be maximized. Eventually the grafted branches will become exhausted and weak. Several times certain varieties of seedless grapes were close to extinction and had to be transferred indoors where they were carefully treated until strong again. For this reason, seedless groves and vineyards are maintained through careful pruning and thinning. This is also why seedless fruit is generally more expensive than the regular, seedy varieties.

Whatever happened to Punkinhead?

Punkinhead was the creation of the Eaton's advertising department for the 1948 Christmas season in Toronto. He was a funny little bear with a mop of orange hair that gave him his name. According to the copywriters at Eaton's, Santa Claus brought along a group of clowns to visit one Christmas. Unfortunately, one of the clowns was sick and could not make the trip. The clown's hat was a perfect fit for Punkinhead, so he filled in as a Christmas clown, became a mascot of the Eaton's-sponsored Christmas parade, and everyone lived happily ever after. At least, until the early 1980s, when Eaton's gave up sponsorship of Toronto's Santa Claus parade and Punkinhead.

Punkinhead was popular through the 1950s, when he starred on records, in colouring books, on souvenirs, and on other promotional items aimed at children. His star faded in the 1960s, but he made a comeback in 1975 and led the Santa Claus parade until 1982. Punkinhead, now retired, resides in the official archives of the Government of Ontario.

How strong was the sentiment in Newfoundland to join the United States instead of Canada?

Canada's youngest province joined the Dominion of Canada in 1949, but not without a few bitter battles. Newfoundland was a separate dominion with its own responsible government until it went bankrupt in 1932. The British stepped in at that time, and from 1933 until 1949, the Government of Newfoundland was run by a commission of seven appointees. Three commissioners were from Newfoundland, and the other three commissioners and the Governor were from Britain. All were appointed by Britain.

After World War II, it came time to make a decision. Newfoundland's future was to be determined by referendum. There were to be three choices: confederation with Canada, a return to responsible self-government, or continued commission government.

A fourth option was proposed in November of 1947. The Party for Economic Union with the United States wanted, as its name implied, Newfoundland and Labrador to form economic ties with the United States, yet maintain responsible government. The party was lead by Chesley A. Crosbie, father of John Crosbie, the colourful member of the Mulroney cabinet.

Some historians have characterized the debate as a close race for all sides, but Crosbie was unable to have his fourth option included on the referendum ballot. The idea didn't catch on with the Americans, either. Peter Neary wrote in his book *Newfoundland in the North Atlantic World 1929-1949* , "if ever there was a suitor whose attentions were unwanted, it was Crosbie's party."

But Newfoundlanders weren't eager to join Canada, either. It took two referenda before a choice was made. Confederation beat out responsible government by only 7,000 votes out of about 150,000 ballots cast.

Where do ants go in winter?

As winter approaches, ants move deep into their nests, where food that has been collected all summer has been stored in special chambers. Only the top few inches of top soil freeze. Beneath this layer of frozen soil, life goes on in the colony.

The size of ant nests varies from just one chamber of a few inches in diameter to vast networks that extend 40 feet underground and house a population of up to 10,000,000 ants. North American ant communities can consist of 12 or more main nests connected by tunnels. The entire colony can cover an area the size of a tennis court.

As the ground thaws out in spring, the ants work their way out of the nests and begin the task of gathering food for the next winter.

Why is a dashboard called a dashboard?

The dashboard, or instrument panel of a car, traces its name back long before the invention of the automobile. In the days of the horse-drawn carriage, there was a problem with mud and dirt being kicked up by the horses as they "dashed." And riders of one-horse open sleighs, of course, are known to dash through the snow, laughing all the way. They wouldn't be laughing if snow was kicked in their faces.

The dashboard, as it was originally conceived, was the front part of a carriage or sleigh, usually made of wood or leather, designed to protect its occupants from whatever the horse was stepping in. In the earliest cars, which were closely modelled after the carriages, the dashboard was in the same location. The name stuck, even after the meaning became obsolete.

How many people have killed themselves by jumping off the Golden Gate Bridge?

People began jumping off San Francisco's Golden Gate Bridge almost as soon as it was completed in 1937. Between 1937 and 1990, 850 people have jumped from the bridge to their deaths. In an average year, 17 people will take the plunge.

This figure is based largely on the number of people actually seen jumping off the bridge and the number of bodies recovered. In some cases, a number is added to the official tally if a suicide note, an abandoned car, or other evidence is found, but only after thorough investigation. There have been a number of faked jumps by people attempting to pull an insurance scam or to escape the law.

The bridge is a popular spot for those serious about their suicidal intentions because of easy access and the low chance of survival. Impact with the water after the 91-metre drop is like hitting a concrete wall at 140 kilometres an hour. Only 17 suicide attempts in the bridge's history have failed.

Why is there no letter Q on the telephone dial?

There was a time when the letters on the telephone dial were an important part of telephone numbers. Until the 1960s, telephone exchanges had names. The first two or three letters in the exchange name were part of the telephone number. For example, if you lived in the Franklin exchange area, your number might have been F-R-A-1-2-1-2. Q was not used because there are so few words with Q as one of the first three letters. Q is further limited because it's almost always followed by the same letter, U.

Z appeared on some phones between 1930 and 1960 but was rarely used, so it was finally dropped as well.

The number 1 had no letters assigned to it because of technical problems with early phones. When the handset was lifted from these phones, the receiver jiggled and caused an unwanted impulse. That impulse was sent through the system as a dialed 1, so the system was designed so that no calls could begin with 1. Later, after the problem was solved, 1 was used to signal a long distance call.

Zero has always been used for calling the operator, and therefore could not be used as the first digit of a phone number.

Even though exchange names are no longer widely used, telephone pads still have letters. Businesses and other organizations often find it useful to have a number that translates into an easily-remembered word.

Who invented eyeglasses?

The use of glass as a visual aid goes back to about 1000 BC. Archaeologists have found glass lenses in the ruins of the ancient city of Nineveh, located in northern Iraq. Scientists believe the lenses were used by scribes drawing minute hieroglyphics.

English scholar Roger Bacon studied the optical properties of glass in the 13th century. He noted that convex lenses could improve vision, and sent an example of his lens to the Pope.

Although the evidence is not conclusive, it appears the first person to make eyeglasses was Salvino Armato, a glass-blower who lived in Pisa in the late thirteenth century. The innovation caught on quickly. Venice was the centre of the European glass industry, and by 1300 craftsmen were adding eyeglasses to their range of products. The first glasses were used for reading and close-up work and were considered a great boon since they extended the working life of those losing their vision to old age. Concave lenses, which corrected nearsightedness, were not considered useful and were not introduced until the 15th century.

The frames of glasses have also changed over the years. Rigid arms that loop over the ears were not added until the 18th century. Originally, frames were merely balanced on the nose, restricting movement and breathing. Some early wearers held the frames in place with leather straps tied around their heads or to their ears.

What do food labels that say "may contain..." really mean?

By law, the labels on prepared food packages must include a list of ingredients. But some labels say, for example, "may contain olive oil or palm oil." Manufacturers are allowed to include "may contain" on their labels under the federal Food and Drug Regulation Act.

A manufacturer may order similar supplies from different sources at different times, according to cost and availability. The act gives such manufacturers the flexibility to change ingredients that don't materially change their product. With this leeway, the product can be labelled with one all-purpose label without the company having to incur the cost of changing labels with every batch. A manufacturer must have a legitimate case for using "may contain," however, and it may not be used to disguise the product's actual ingredients. A consumer can assume the product contains one of the choices listed under "may contain."

Why do singers lose their accents when they sing?

There are several physiological elements that contribute to uttering a sound. Balancing these elements is different for singing and speaking. Pronunciation of vowels, for example, is an important characteristic of spoken accents. When a singer switches from speech to song, however, the vowels are drawn out for maximum resonance. Because there is a limited number of ways to achieve this resonance, the pronunciation of vowels when singing has become standardized.

A singer also places more emphasis on the diaphragm for projection, but returns to the larynx for speech. The larynx allows a greater variety of sounds, and it is this selection of sound, through years of social conditioning, that makes one accent different from another.

The timing and pace of spoken words also influences an accent. When singers sing, they must give up their own speech patterns to the demands of the music. This is most necessary with rigorous classical music, and least necessary with songs that are more like spoken verse, such as those sung in the British music hall.

Through deliberate control of these factors, or through a change in social environment, an individual's spoken accent can also be altered.

How much paper can be obtained from the average-sized tree?

Such a question is abstract, of course, and the answer is dependent on a number of conditions. The weight and quality of the paper desired will affect how much can be produced from a fixed volume of pulp.

In the pulp business, a tree's volume is measured by its diameter at the stump. A tree with a wide diameter is taller and has more volume than a tree with a smaller diameter. Since the wood is reduced to pulp, all that matters is the total volume.

The pulp from a tree with a stump diameter of 12 inches produces enough paper to print 40 average-sized hard-cover books. A tree with a stump diameter of eight inches, which would be about 40 feet tall, produces enough pulp for 1500 rolls of two-ply toilet paper. It thus takes roughly one-half an inch of cross-section of that tree to manufacture one roll of toilet paper. Give or take a few sheets.

What is the origin of the expression "on cloud nine"?

"On cloud nine," the phrase used to describe a feeling of euphoria, is based on the terminology of the US Weather Bureau. There are nine different types of clouds, rated from one to nine. The ninth type is the cumulonimbus cloud, the cloud we might see on a hot summer afternoon. The cumulonimbus cloud is a thundercloud that builds itself up to 30 or 40 thousand feet high and looks like it reaches to the top of the world.

The term developed into a catch phrase during the 1950s on a radio program called *The Johnny Dowler Show*. Whenever the protagonist was knocked unconscious, he was said to have been transported to Cloud Nine.

How did the name John become a euphemism for "toilet"?

"John" is one of the older of the many terms used in "loo" of toilet. John and Cousin John's go back to 15th century England. They probably come from Jack, Jake, and Jake's house, which were also alternate names for the outhouse. Jake, a derivative of John, was used as a derogatory generic name meaning a country bumpkin.

What is the origin of the 1960s civil rights theme song *We Shall Overcome*?

We Shall Overcome has its roots in spiritual music. Reverend C. Albert Tindley wrote and published a hymn, *I'll Overcome Some Day*, in 1900. There are many similarities between the lyrics of this hymn and those of the song that became the civil rights anthem, but the music was different.

The melody of *We Shall Overcome* goes back even further. The first four bars of the song are recognizable in a hymn called *O Sanctissima*. The hymn was first written down in 1795, but it may be much older.

Another song, also titled *I'll Overcome Some Day*, was published on May 1st, 1945. According to the sheet music, the song is a Negro song with original words by Atron Twigg and revised lyrics and music by Kenneth Morris.

Two days later, Roberta Martin published a song called *I'll Be Like Him Some Day*. The last 12 bars of this song are similar to those in *We Shall Overcome*. The words to Martin's song include the line, "I'll overcome some day."

The CIO Food and Tobacco Workers in Charleston, South Carolina, sang a version of the civil rights song during a strike in October of 1945, singing "We will overcome." Two of the strikers later attended a labour workshop in Tennessee and sang it to their union brothers. The song was picked up by Zilphia Horton, who taught it to others.

Pete Seeger heard the song in 1950 and began singing it in the American north, changing the title line to "We shall overcome."

During the early civil rights movement, white folk singer Guy Carawan began teaching Seeger's version to black students. Soon it was heard at demonstrations throughout the south.

As a result of the complicated development of *We Shall Overcome*, its creation is credited as "adapted by Zilphia Horton, Frank Hamilton, Guy Carawan, and Pete Seeger."

How does putting a mothball in your gasoline tank improve the octane rating?

The urban myth that spiking a tank of gasoline with mothballs increases the octane rating and the mileage is based on fact. But it's not very practical.

A fuel's octane rating is a measurement of how much energy it releases when it is burned. Substances that improve combustion efficiency increase the energy released during burning and therefore increase the octane rating of a fuel.

Mothballs are made of naphthalene, a relatively light hydrocarbon that burns more efficiently than most of the heavier hydrocarbons found in gasoline. Adding mothballs will therefore increase the octane rating of gasoline. But one or two mothballs wouldn't make a measurable difference to a tankful of fuel. To improve the octane level of regular unleaded gasoline to that of a premium unleaded, one would have to add about a pound of mothballs. The result would be a dirty engine and spark plugs clogged with carbon.

Why do men have nipples?

All human bodies are made up of a basic structure that includes the parts needed by both sexes, such as the heart, liver, fingers, bones, etc. That basic structure also includes a few parts that may never become active, such as mammary glands on men.

The only absolute differences between the male and female body are the reproductive organs, which are known as the primary sexual characteristics. All other differences are secondary sexual characteristics, such as breasts, facial hair, and muscle mass, and are shared to some extent by both sexes. It is up to the body's hormonal balance to determine whether the mammary glands will develop or remain dormant.

When a child reaches puberty, hormones activate the development of the secondary sexual characteristics. Normally, estrogen in a girl stimulates the growth of breasts, and testosterone causes a boy's chin to grow hair. But a hormonal imbalance can lead to abnormal growth of dormant secondary sexual characteristics. This is what happens to women who grow a mustache. There have also been cases of men being treated with estrogen for prostate cancer who lactate, or produce milk.

Where does the term "OK" come from?

In the late 1830s, it was an American fad to play with the language. The fad began in 1838, when the Boston Globe was making deliberately excessive use of abbreviations.

Big shots were "OFM,"our fine men. "NG" meant no go, and "SP" stood for small potatoes. Many of the abbreviations were of words with fanciful alternate spellings: "NS" was "nuff said," and "OW" was "oll wright." "OK" was first published by the Globe in March 1839, and meant "oll korrect."

This fad of using unusual abbreviations spread briefly to New York City and New Orleans, but quickly died out. "OK" lingered on longer than most of the other abbreviations.

Supporters of presidential candidate Martin Van Buren adopted "OK" at the Democratic convention of 1840. Van Buren, a native of Kinderhook, New York, was known as Old Kinderhook. As "OK" caught on, Van Buren's opponents and the press came up with their own definitions; Out of Kash, Out of Kredit, Orfully Konfused, and Often Kontradicts were among the kinder epithets. By the end of the campaign, the expression was firmly entrenched in the language.

Who is Dr. Seuss?

Dr. Seuss, one of the most widely recognized names in modern children's literature, is the pen name of Theodore Seuss Geisel. He was born in Springfield, Massachusetts in 1904, and later received formal training in art.

Geisel's taste for fantasy goes at least as far back as the 1930s, when he was a regular cartoonist and writer for the college humour magazines of the era, such as Judge and the original Life. His series of magazine and newspaper ads for an insecticide made "Quick, Henry, the Flit!" a national catchphrase. The title of a recently-published collection of his magazine and advertising work reveals Geisel's interest in language: *The Tough Coughs As He Ploughs the Dough*.

Geisel wrote his first book for children, *The Cat in the Hat*, in response to an article he saw in Life magazine. The story criticized the books used in schools to teach children to read. As Dr. Seuss, Geisel strove to create a book that would be as different as possible from the bland Dick and Jane readers used at the time. He felt children would want to read to the end his stories of fanciful creatures speaking in nonsense verse.

One of Geisel's lasting contributions is *The Grinch Who Stole Christmas*. The Grinch has become as permanent a cultural Christmas icon as Scrooge himself.

In 1986, after many years of writing books for children, Dr. Seuss published a book especially for grandparents, titled *You're Only Old Once*.

Geisel was awarded a Pulitzer Prize Citation for his contribution to children's literature in 1984.

Why are horseshoes thought to be lucky?

The Greeks, who invented horseshoes, considered the horseshoe lucky because it resembled the crescent moon, a symbol of fertility and good fortune.

But for Christian cultures, the credit goes to St. Dunstan, a blacksmith who became the Archbishop of Canterbury in 959 AD. One day, a gentleman visited Dunstan's shop and ordered a pair of horseshoes to be attached to his own suspiciously cloven feet. Recognizing the stranger to be Satan, Dunstan agreed to do the job, but claimed that to do the task properly, he would have to shackle the customer. The Devil fell for the ruse, and his feet were tortured until the blacksmith extracted a promise from Satan that he would never enter a house that had a horseshoe above the door.

Horseshoes eventually moved to the door itself, where they also served as a knockers. Even today, some door knockers are designed like a horseshoe.

Horseshoes have also been used to ward off other sources of evil, from witches to fairies. Witches rode brooms because they feared horses, and any reminder of horses was thought to keep them away. For example, a horseshoe was affixed to the lid of a witch's coffin to discourage resurrection.

It is very important that horseshoes are hung on a door or over a door frame with the ends pointing up; otherwise the luck will spill out.

Can businesses legally refuse to accept certain denominations of currency?

Businesses that are open late at night, such as gas stations and convenience stores, often post a sign saying they will not accept bills above a certain denomination, usually $20 or $50. This is to reduce the risk of robbery by limiting the amount of money in the till. But since paper currency is actually a check drawn on the government's reserves, and since the courts have determined that all checks bearing the legal requirements must be accepted, it follows that a bill of any denomination must be accepted.

However, the "pay to the bearer on demand" rule only applies to banks. Everybody else is free to reject any form of payment they wish. The Currency Act places limits on the use of coinage for large payments, but the Act makes no mention of paper money in that respect. The Bank of Canada also has no policy to cover the possibility of its currency not being accepted.

No one has gone to court to question the right of a business to not accept large bills even if they are able, or to accept only exact change, for that matter.

What causes hair to turn grey?

The 100,000 hairs on the average human head are coloured by a pigment called melanin. As a person grows older, the hair follicles produce less and less melanin. The space in the hair shaft that had been occupied by the pigment eventually becomes filled with air. When light reflects off these air spaces, the hair has the appearance of being grey.

Heredity is the main factor that determines when in a lifetime hair will turn grey. Grey hair may also be caused by scalp conditions or a vitamin deficiency. It is also believed that stress can slowly turn hair grey, but how this process works is unknown.

What is the origin of the phrase "three sheets to the wind"?

"Three sheets to the wind" is just one of dozens of expressions used to describe a state of drunkenness. The phrase comes from a nautical term that means to lose control of a ship.

Sheets are the lines of a ship, or the ropes controlling the sails. The main sheet controls the main sail, and the two jib sheets control the foresail, or front sail. If a sailor lost control of the sheets to the wind, he lost control of the vessel. Therefore, if he was so drunk that he was out of control, he was said to be "three sheets to the wind."

What is the origin of Uncle Sam?

Uncle Sam, the American icon of national character in his star-spangled suit and top hat, was originally a meatpacker from New York. Samuel Wilson was a patriot in his own right. As an eight-year-old, he was the drummer boy who alerted his village of Menotomy, later known as Arlington, to the advancing redcoats. That was the same morning in 1775 when Paul Revere made his historic ride through Lexington.

Sam's boyhood pal, John Chapman, was another figure destined to become an American folk hero. Chapman would later be known as Johnny Appleseed.

At age 14, Wilson joined the army and fought in the revolutionary war. After the war, he went into the meat-packing business, and his reputation for fair business practices earned him the nickname Uncle Sam.

During the War of 1812, Wilson had a government contract to provide the military with pork and beef. To indicate which crates in the packing plant were destined for the army, Wilson marked them with a large "U.S." At that time, this abbreviation for United States was not very common.

One version of the story says that when government inspectors visited the plant, they asked a worker what the letters stood for. Not sure himself, he joked that they must refer to his employer, Uncle Sam. According to another version, soldiers in Troy, New York, recognized the crates from Wilson's slaughterhouse and dubbed the supplies "Uncle Sam's." Either way, all government-issue supplies were eventually said to come from Uncle Sam.

Uncle Sam, the personification of the United States, first saw print in the newspapers of New England in the 1820s. Throughout the rest of the century, cartoonists and illustrators modified Uncle Sam's appearance. The most widely-recognized interpretations of Uncle Sam are probably those of Thomas Nast and James Montgomery Flagg. Nast was the Civil War and Reconstruction period cartoonist who modelled his tall, determined Uncle Sam after Abraham Lincoln; Flagg painted the World War I "I Want You" poster.

The United States Congress passed a resolution in 1961 saluting Samuel Wilson as the person who inspired one of America's national symbols.

What is the origin of the phrase "brand new"?

"Brand new" goes back at least to the Middle Ages. It referred to an object of metal or pottery that had been retrieved from the fire where it had hardened. "Brand" comes from the Old English *baernan*, which means "to burn." Shakespeare uses the phrase "fire new" in *Richard III*.

In more modern times, the brand became the mark burned onto cattle to identify ownership. It has also come to refer to any mark or name a business uses to identify itself or its products.

Why are moths drawn to bright lights at night?

Moths, being nocturnal insects, don't require light to see, but they do use it for orientation. Moths orient their flight paths to the moon. Because the moon is so far away, its angle relative to the moth never changes.

Sometimes, however, a moth tries to orient its flight path according to a nearby light. Because earth-bound light sources are closer than the moon, the moth's angle relative to the the light source changes as the moth moves. The result is an erratic flight pattern that sends the moth in a spiral towards the light. If the light source is a fire, the moth will often fly close enough to the flames to become singed.

Whether a moth will be confused by a porch-light depends on the intensity of the light from the moon. Thus, fewer moths hang around porchlights on nights with a full moon.

What does the *S* in Harry S Truman stand for?

The *S* in Harry S Truman stands for S. The former President's middle name is S. Truman's parents gave the unusual middle name to their son to placate both grandfathers. The grandfathers' names were Shippe Truman and Solomon Young.

As Truman became a public figure, the proper treatment of his name became controversial among those who keep track of this sort of thing. Grammarians of the day could not agree on whether the *S* should be followed by a period. Was the *S* an initial without a name, or was it a name unto itself, and, if so, wouldn't the initial of S be S, and how could you tell the difference?

The usually Plain-Speaking Harry wasn't much help, either. He signed his name with and without the period.

How long will a videotape last?

Videotape was first developed in the mid-1950s, and it soon revolutionized the way in which studio television programs were produced. There were several attempts to sell the consumer market on the idea of a home video recorder, but it did not catch on until 1975, when the Betamax was introduced by Sony. Video cameras have since become so practical and easy to use that, for better or worse, home movies are even bigger now than they were at their peak when everyone made flickering silent films thirty years ago.

Nobody yet knows how long a videotape will last. Many of the programs recorded when videotape was introduced still exist with little sign of deterioration, and videotape has gone through tremendous improvements since then.

However, a tape's life can be greatly shortened through careless treatment and storage. Tapes should always be kept in their plastic or cardboard cases to keep out dust. Tapes should never be stored next to speakers or other sources of magnetic fields. The tape inside the plastic shell should never be touched.

For long-term storage, the cassette should sit on its side, either upright like a book or sideways, so that the edge of the tape inside does not bear the weight of the entire reel.

Although a tape will wear out eventually through repeated use, most reputable brands are good for at least 500 plays.

When did junk mail start?

Direct mail advertising, the term preferred by its practitioners, goes back to at least the 1770s when Benjamin Franklin printed and distributed through the mail a catalogue of 600 books available through his press. In Canada, handbills published by patent medicine sellers were distributed via the post office as early as 1840. The class act in Canadian direct mail advertising was the Eaton's catalogue, first published in 1884.

Direct mail advertising is an important source of revenue for the post office. In 1933, the Assistant Deputy Postmaster General was advising Canadian businesses to "plan now to use the mails for better sales." The Royal Canadian Post Office even published a booklet at the time called *Six Keys to Better Business*, in which it declared, "the Canadian Post Office, realizing that its revenue is directly dependent on general business conditions, has considered it good policy to do everything to stimulate business generally."

In 1989, Canada Post earned $200,000,000 delivering junk mai... oops, direct mail advertising, which makes up about 40 per cent of the mail the post office moves. That's about 2,730,000,000 pieces every year.

Why are unemployment benefits called "pogey"?

The word "pogey" may have evolved from the English word *pogue*, which was first used in 1525 to mean "help" or "support." *Pogue* comes from the Italian word *appoggio* which means "leaning place" or "support."

"Pogey" first appeared in print in 1891 in the United States. It meant a hostel or poorhouse. Hobos adopted the word in the 1930s as a term for a place where the unemployed were welcome to stay. When the houses disappeared, pogey came to mean money paid out to the unemployed.

These days, in theory, unemployment benefits are not paid out by the government but are the payback of contributions made earlier by the employee. In a 1961 article on pogey and unemployment insurance benefits, Maclean's magazine said "today unemployment insurance benefits are often referred to as pogey. But pogey in the depths of the Depression meant something as different from the present unemployment insurance as panhandling is from drawing money from your bank account."

What were the First and Second Reichs?

The First Reich began in 913 AD, when Otto I became king of Germany. The First Reich is more commonly referred to as the Holy Roman Empire. As the saying goes, it was neither holy, Roman, nor an empire. After the collapse of Charlemagne's Roman Empire, Europe was divided into what became France, Italy, and Germany. In 936, Otto came to the aid of the pope, who was having trouble with some Italian princes. After subduing the princes, Otto overthrew the Pope himself. The papacy later regained its independence, but Otto's kingdom kept the name of Holy Roman Empire. The empire was a loose confederation of principalities and kingdoms held together by the Habsburg emperors. The Holy Roman Empire, the First Reich, collapsed in 1803 because of conflict between Prussia and Austria within the empire and because of instability caused by the French Revolution. The Habsburg line continued to rule the Austrian and Austro-Hungarian empires.

The Second Reich began in 1871, after a renewed drive to unify the German states and the German victory in the Franco-Prussian war. The chief architect of Germany's rise from relative weakness to world power within one generation was Otto von Bismarck. Both the Second Reich and the Austrian empire came to an end with the surrender of Germany and Austria after World War I.

Why do they make screws with different kinds of heads?

The slotted screw head has been around for hundreds of years. It is the easiest and cheapest screw to manufacture. However, because of the open sides of the slot, the blade of the screwdriver can easily slip out. The slot-head screw is commonly used for wood screws.

The Phillips head is a European design. Its cross-shaped head will not let the screwdriver slip, and it is easier to apply torque, or more pressure on the threads, as it is twisted. The Phillips head is thought to be the most aesthetic design, and it is commonly used where the screw is visible.

The Robertson head is a Canadian design developed early in this century. Inventor Peter L. Robertson of Milton, Ontario was working on a new multi-purpose tool in 1907. His slot screwdriver slipped and cut into his hand. The experience led him to design a head with a square hole. The head allows greater torque to be applied and allows the screw to stay in place on the screwdriver, an advantage when working in a tight space.

There are several other types of screws designed for specific tasks. One such screw is the torx, which allows even more torque. This screw does not come out easily, however, and it is expensive to produce. For safety reasons, it is used for such products as cars, and its installation requires a special tool.

Why does snow in the mountains sometimes have a reddish tinge?

During the summer months, a pink algae called *Chlamydomonas nivalis* comes out of dormancy and lives in the water between snow crystals. This algae is very particular; it grows only in water trapped in snow, and only if the temperature is above zero degrees Celsius. These ideal conditions must exist for at least a month for the algae to survive. Thus, the algae is seen only in summer, and only at higher elevations. At the lower altitudes, snow melts too quickly for the algae to develop.

As the pockets of water containing the algae become more concentrated through the summer, the snow turns red. The algae also gives off a faint odour like watermelon.

Chlamydomonas nivalis is located at the bottom of a unique food chain. Snow worms eat the algae, and rose finches then eat the worms.

Why is depression called the blues?

There are several theories to explain the term "feeling the blues." One comes from Blue Monday. Blue Monday was not originally a dreary occasion, but rather a day for revelry and pleasure. For centuries it was the custom to decorate churches with blue hangings on the Monday before the beginning of Lent. In order to make up for the anticipated restrictions of the upcoming Lenten period, a great feast was held on Blue Monday. Eating and drinking went on all night. By the 16th century, the holiday was celebrated to such excess that the practice was abolished by law. Because Blue Monday was followed by that morning-after feeling, blue came to be used to describe any depression.

Another theory also comes from the hangover. After a night of boozing, people would wake up in a state of delirium and profess to having seen blue devils in their dreams.

Finally, back in mercantilist times, Monday was the day when sailors were flogged for their wrongdoings during the week. They were beaten black and blue, and feeling blue was the term used to describe how the sailors felt for the rest of the day.

How did the tradition of the wishing well come about?

The tradition of throwing coins into wishing wells comes from pre-Christian Europe. The worship of water was a pagan practice. Water was revered because it was essential to life. Water was also mysterious to the pagans because its movement was unpredictable. Water could also destroy people and places through flooding. It was believed that a divine force inhabited springs, flowing rivers, and waterfalls.

Believers went to wells to pray. Sacrifices, which might include offerings of money, were made to the spirits of the water to curry favour, find answers to problems, and cure ailments.

Certain wells dealt only with specific concerns. In Bisbey, Oxford, for example, there was a well where those with eye problems went in search of a cure. Another well, called St. Aelian's Well, specialized in consoling broken-hearted maidens. At this well, the women threw pins instead of money. There are still heaps of pins lying at the bottom of St. Aelian's well.

How many times can a sheet of paper be recycled?

The number of times a sheet of paper can be recycled depends on its original quality. Low-grade paper like newsprint can usually be recycled only once. Higher grade paper like magazine stock can be recycled two or three times into progressively lower grades of paper.

New pulp must be added to recycled pulp during the recycling process. Each time paper is recycled, the paper fibres get smaller and weaker. New pulp is added to restore at least some strength. There is also a certain amount of sludge left behind each time the paper is recycled, so there is some loss of the original sheet by attrition. By the time a sheet of paper has been recycled several times, there is very little of it still in the cycle.

Why do horses run counter-clockwise around a racetrack?

Horses have a natural tendency to lean to the left when they run in a circle. Humans have the same tendency. When running, we tend to lead with the left foot and pull to the left.

Horse trainers put the horse's left lean to good use. During training and practice runs, the horses run clockwise. During races, however, the horses run counter-clockwise. Thus, when the jockey turns his horse around, the horse knows by conditioning that the race is on and it's time to really burn the oats.

The majority of racetracks around the world run counter-clockwise, but some tracks in Britain, Australia, and Germany run clockwise. Horses from other countries scheduled to race on clockwise tracks are sent well in advance of the race day so that they have time to get used to running in the opposite direction.

How is caffeine removed from coffee?

There are several ways to decaffeinate coffee, but most coffee companies now use the steam method. To remove the caffeine from coffee beans, companies steam the raw beans with water, which causes them to swell up. During this process, the caffeine moves to the outer surface of the beans. The beans are then immersed in carbon dioxide, which extracts the caffeine from the surface of the beans. Once decaffeinated, the beans are dried, roasted, ground, and packaged for sale.

Why are barns traditionally painted red?

Even in the early days, farmers had to watch their pennies. Farmers had to make paint for their barns using the kinds of things you'd find around a farm. The common formula for barn paint was five pounds of iron oxide, or ochre, added to one gallon of linseed oil to produce enough orange-red wash to cover the barn.

Not all farmers had to rely on home-grown paint, however. The railways used to paint their cars a rust-red, and they often had plenty of paint left over. Some of the farmers who lived along the rail lines were able to scrounge up enough donated paint to paint the barn for next to nothing.

Who decides what our commemorative stamps will commemorate?

There are two types of postage stamp. Definitive stamps are issued for everyday use. They are the common, straight-forward stamps that bear the portrait of the Queen, the flag, and so on. Functional, but not very interesting.

The other type of stamp, the commemorative issue, commemorates a person or event, and a great deal of effort goes into its preparation. Each commemorative is issued for a limited time only; Canada issues about 15 commemoratives each year.

Canada Post has a research department that finds topics for commemorative stamp series. Many commemoratives are inspired by the anniversaries of great moments in history or the birth of historical figures. Other subjects include cultural themes, such as Inuit art, and national events, such as the Olympics and Expo. The department also fields suggestions from the public.

The research department submits a list of recommended topics to the Stamp Advisory Committee, which makes the final choices. The committee then commissions artists to come up with appropriate designs, all of which are subject to approval.

This drawn-out process sounds expensive, but it actually pays off because the commemoratives are highly prized by stamp collectors. Stamps that are purchased but not used as postage have a high profit margin.

Philatelists worldwide like to collect Canadian stamps because they present aspects of our nation well and are of a high quality.

How fast did the silktrains run?

From the 1880s to the 1930s, silktrains ran across Canada from the ports of Vancouver to Quebec and Ontario with their precious cargo headed for American markets. The trains were famous for their breakneck speeds.

In 1890, the Canadian Pacific Railway cornered the lucrative silk transportation market by commissioning three modern ships to haul the silk, and silkworms still in their cocoons, across the Pacific. The ships could make the trip from the Orient in ten days, a week faster than the competition. At the Vancouver docks, the cargo was loaded onto specially-designed railway cars. These cars were half the length of regular box cars and had flared wheels, which allowed them to be pulled at high speeds. A train of 6 to 15 cars carried up to $10 million worth of product.

With cargo of that value, time was money. The CPR insured the cargo at an hourly rate. As well, silk was listed on the commodities exchanges, and unstable prices meant that it had to get to market as soon as possible. At one point, the rush was so great that a train carrying King George VI was shunted off to a side track to let a silktrain pass by at full speed. The crews of the silktrains viewed the demand for speed as a challenge and tried to create new records for the steam-powered trains. One of those known records is over 60 miles per hour between Brandon and Winnipeg. There is another, unconfirmed, claim of a train reaching 85 miles per hour on its way out of Moose Jaw.

The decline of the silk trade during the

Depression made the silktrain runs unprofitable. The last train ran in 1939.

Why isn't Earth named after Greek and Roman mythological figures, like the other planets?

The tradition of naming planets after the gods goes back long before civilization's thinkers realized that the earth was not the centre of the universe. They did not think Earth was a planet.

The ancient civilizations thought the movement of the planets was an indicator of the gods' activities, so the heavenly bodies were named after their respective proprietors. But to the Greeks, Earth also was a part of the cosmic drama. Earth was known to the Greeks as Gaea, Gaia, or Ge. The goddess Gaea was both mother and wife of Uranus, or heaven.

Naming the planets after the ancient gods is a tradition that astronomers have carried into modern times. The furthest planet in our system, discovered in the 1930s, was named after Pluto, the god of Hades.

Our own name for planet Earth comes from an Anglo-Saxon word that means "that which is all around us."

Where does the hockey term "hat trick" come from?

If a hockey player scores three goals in a game, he is said to have scored a hat trick. The term comes from the somewhat more pastoral game of cricket. If a cricket player made three uninterrupted wickets, that is, if he scored three times in a row without another player scoring in between, then the other players took up a collection on his behalf. They passed around the hat.

Other sports also have hat tricks, but the term is most closely associated with hockey. Originally, a hat trick was achieved when a hockey player scored three consecutive goals with no one from either team scoring in between. Over time, however, the definition of the term changed, and a hat trick is now achieved when a player scores three goals in one game. The feat of scoring three consecutive goals is now referred to as a natural hat trick.

Two of the more unusual records in National Hockey League history involve hat tricks. In an overtime period in 1934, before the days of sudden death overtime, Ken Dougherty of the Toronto Maple Leafs scored three goals to defeat the Ottawa Senators. It is the only overtime hat trick on the books. In 1952, Bill Mosienko of the Chicago Blackhawks had the fastest hat trick, scoring three goals in 21 seconds.

What is the origin of the wedding custom of tossing the bride's garter?

The tradition of throwing the bride's garter is derived from an old English ritual known as the flinging of the stocking. Wedding guests invaded the bridal chamber and stole the stockings of the bride and the groom. Women stole the groom's stockings, and men went after the bride's. The guests then took turns flinging the stockings at the faces of the couple. The person who first hit one or the other on the nose would be the next to marry.

By the 14th century, the garter holding up the bride's stocking was so highly prized that guests wouldn't wait for the wedding night — they rushed the bride at the altar and tried to take it off.

Today, the groom usually removes the garter with the cooperation of the bride and tosses it over his shoulder to a crowd of single men. The bachelor who catches it is said to be the next one to marry.

Why are highways called highways?

The *high* in highway comes from the Old English word *heah*, which had several related meanings. They included chief, principle, main, special, great, upward, magnitude, and tall. *Heah* was also used to describe mountains and cliffs.

Several of the definitions apply to the highways of today. The one that applied then meant literally a high way. A pathway connecting different parts of the country often ran over hills rather than through valleys. This was an advantage for travellers, since from a higher vantage point it was easier to avoid robbers. And there were enough bandits around to justify their own name: highwaymen.

What is the world's oldest inhabited city?

The oldest city still inhabited is Jericho, located in the occupied territories of the West Bank. Radio-carbon dating of ancient artifacts places the founding of the walled city at about 7800 BC. Archaeologists believe the population of the city was about 3,000 at that time. Today, about 70,000 people live in Jericho.

The oldest capital city in the world is not far from Jericho. The capital of Syria, Damascus, has been continuously inhabited since 2500 BC.

Why do some foods in a microwave oven heat from the inside and some from the outside?

Microwave ovens heat food by exciting water molecules in the food; that is, by making the water molecules move faster. This movement produces heat, which cooks the food. The molecules stop being excited as soon as the microwaves cease, but the heat transfer from the hot outer edge to the cooler centre continues for some time. That's why some microwave recipes include "sitting time." Until the heat transfer is complete, the food is still cooking.

A bun or a loaf of bread has very little moisture in it, and hence few water molecules for the microwaves to agitate. What moisture there is in bread is in the middle. The microwaves therefore pass right through the dry outer part of the bread without heating it up, and agitate the water molecules, which are found only in the centre. Thus, bread heats up from the inside out. A food that is moist in the middle and dry on the outside can easily be overcooked since the cooking process cannot be easily monitored.

When did the tradition of lighting cigarette lighters at rock concerts begin?

Go to almost any big-name rock concert and you'll see thousands of flickering lighters in the audience as the lights go down and the show begins. The lighters are usually flicked on again at the end of the concert. This tradition started with concerts by Melanie, who sang her song *Lay Down Candles in the Rain*.

The song was inspired by Melanie's experience as a performer at the Woodstock festival in 1969. Despite the rain at the festival, the sprawling audience was warm and receptive to her music. The second verse of the song is about raising a candle high to keep the cold and darkness away.

When Melanie performed *Lay Down Candles in the Rain* at another concert in mid-1970, the audience responded by flicking their lighters and matches while she sang. It was the audience's way of participating in the performance.

How many bottles of beer will a bushel of barley produce?

Barley intended for beer production is prepared by a maltster. The maltster purchases barley from a local grain elevator, which has paid the farmer about $2.40 a bushel. The maltster steeps the barley in water until it germinates to a desired stage. The germinated barley, now called malt barley, is then kiln-dried for storage until required by the brewmaster. In this process, the barley loses about 20 per cent of its weight, but increases its value to about $9.52 a bushel.

The brewmaster extracts a sugary brown liquid called wort from the malt barley. The wort is then boiled and hops are added. Yeast converts the sugar into carbon dioxide and alcohol, and the final product is beer. The brewery requires one bushel of malt barley to make one Canadian barrel of beer, which is equivalent to 333 bottles.

Why do women swing their arms in a wider arc than men when walking?

Generally, women swing their arms in a wider arc than men when walking, but there are plenty of exceptions either way. It all depends on body structure.

The female pelvis is broader and shallower than the male pelvis, and shoulder width is narrower for females than males. Because of this, the femur, the large bone in the leg, rotates in the hip joint at a different angle in women, causing a greater sway in the hips. Young girls generally do not lift their knees when walking, which exaggerates the hip sway even more.

The narrower female shoulders mean the arms are carried closer to the body. They must therefore swing out further in order to counter-balance the swaying of the hips.

What is the origin of the swastika?

The swastika is one of the most powerfully negative symbols in our culture. It instantly conjures up images of Adolf Hitler and the Third Reich. The impact of the symbol is so strong that books with a swastika on their jackets need no further illustration or text to stand out on store shelves.

But to other cultures, the swastika has had positive meanings. The swastika was used by Hindus, Buddhists, Romans, North American Indians, and other societies as a sign of good fortune. The word *swastika* comes from Sanskrit, meaning "to be good." Called the Wheel of Life by some, it was seen as a symbol for the ongoing forces of nature. With each quarter revolution, the cross with the bent arms looks the same, suggesting that life goes on. Others saw it as a symbol for the sun circling through the sky.

The swastika was brought to the attention of the public in 19th century Germany by the archaeologist Heinrich Schliemann, who wrote about his diggings in Troy and Mycenae in 1870. His discovery of the ancient Aryan use of the symbol appealed to those wishing to go back to the good old days of Aryan supremacy, a theme exploited most successfully by the Nazis.

The cross with the arms bent to the right, suggesting clockwise movement, is the swastika. Its mirror image, with the arms bent to the left, is called the *sauvastika*. In some cultures, the sauvastika represented the swastika's black magic opposite; in others it was just an alternate design and meant exactly the same as the swastika.

Where does the blood come from for operations by veterinarians?

A pet in need of a blood transfusion is in the same position as a human patient waiting for an organ transplant. If blood is available, it will be used, but there are no blood banks for animals.

When a dog or cat is brought in to the vet to be put to sleep, the veterinarian asks the owner if he or she is willing to have some of the pet's blood removed and stored for emergency use. Like human blood, animal blood will keep for only a few weeks, then it must be destroyed. Plasma removed from the blood will last a little longer. There are many more blood types among cats and dogs than there are among humans, but the risk of blood type rejection is much lower, especially for the first transfusion.

How do clams reproduce?

Clams reproduce sexually, but it is hardly the height of romantic savoir faire that keeps the species alive.

Clams are hermaphrodites, meaning that each individual is both male and female. Some other hermaphroditic species can switch their orientation back and forth according to circumstances, but all clams start life as males and become females during their mid-life crises. Some clams switch back to being males, but most stay female for life.

When mating, the male clam shoots his sperm into the water in the general vicinity of a female. In the course of filtering water for food and oxygen, the female ingests the sperm and her eggs are fertilized inside her shell. When the eggs reach a certain point in their development, the female spawns, releasing the eggs into the water.

Why are there holes in the prongs of electrical plugs?

The two flat prongs on an electrical plug are called blades. They fit into the part of an electrical outlet called the receptacle. Inside the receptacle are the wipers.

The wipers are the exposed ends of the household wiring that carries the electrical current. When a plug is inserted into a receptacle, the blades come into contact with the wipers, and the current flows through the plug.

In order to keep the plug firmly in place, each wiper has a small bump on its otherwise smooth surface. The location of the bump matches the hole in the blade so that when the plug is inserted, the bump snaps into the hole.

How are crossword puzzles created?

The crossword puzzle was introduced in the Sunday supplement of the New York World newspaper in 1913. The designer of the crossword, Arthur Wynne, was inspired by Magic Square, a children's word game in which words are arranged vertically and horizontally. Wynne added empty squares and clues so that the player had to deduce the words.

By the early 1920s, crossword puzzles were standard features of almost every American newspaper. In 1924, four crossword puzzle books were on the bestseller lists. Booksellers also experienced phenomenal sales of another type of book: dictionaries.

Today, crossword puzzlemakers each have their own techniques to challenge the skills of their players. Eugene Waleska, creator of the New York Times crossword puzzle, begins with a theme and lists as many words he can think of that loosely fit the theme. Birds, for example, might prompt pigeon-toed, goose-step, and turkey-trot.

Then Waleska starts to fill in the grid with the long words first, avoiding words ending in J or beginning with X. He works first in the lower right corner of the grid, since it is harder to find a word that ends with a certain letter than it is to find a word that begins with a certain letter. Waleska says that when he started in this business, it took him several days to fit the words into a 15x15 square grid. Now it takes less than an hour.

For Waleska, if the words are the heart of the puzzle, then the definitions are its soul. He tries to base his clues on humour, on little-known facts, or to place them in historical context, as in "Lincoln to Douglas" for "foe".

What is the origin of the name John Doe?

The use of John Doe and his pal Richard Roe on legal documents goes back at least to 14th century Britain. There is speculation that the use of John Doe began after the signing of the Magna Carta in 1215. The Magna Carta states that all contracts require witnesses. Prosecutors playing fast and loose with the rules used John Doe and Richard Roe as witnesses when real ones were not available. It is not known if there ever was a real John Doe.

The fraudulent use of the names Doe and Roe eventually evolved into their use to describe unknown people and hypothetical persons. When used in court cases, John Doe was always the plaintiff, and Richard Roe always the defendant. Since women had few rights in the courts of the day, it is likely that Jane Doe did not enter the scene until much later.

Why is the goose-step named after geese?

The goose-step is a military step in which the legs are kept stiff and the thigh is brought up to a right angle to the body. The march is most closely associated with the Prussian and German armies, but has also been used by Russian, Polish, and Italian forces.

The unnatural movement of the step requires a great deal of discipline if it is to be executed well. Armies adopted the goose-step as a means of encouraging discipline. A well-drilled regiment of men was supposed to look extremely dignified, but during World Wars I and II, the goose-step was a constant target of ridicule by the Allies.

But the goose-step is not named for the awkward waddle of the goose. The name comes from the habit geese have of walking in single file, like a row of soldiers. Even if the lead goose leads an erratic course, the others follow the same path, displaying a kind of discipline.

When did Sherlock Holmes start wearing an Inverness cape and deerstalker hat?

The distinctive Inverness cape and deerstalker hat are instantly recognizable as the uniform of Sherlock Holmes. But nowhere does Holmes' creator, Sir Arthur Conan Doyle, describe Holmes wearing these articles of clothing.

The Inverness cape comes from Inverness, Scotland. It was designed for hunters. Because it was sleeveless, hunters had more freedom of movement, yet the garment was warm. Doyle mentions Holmes wearing a dark grey cloak, but the Inverness was a plaid tweed.

The first illustrator of the Sherlock Holmes adventures, Sydney Paget, gave Holmes his characteristic cloak. It appeared on the cover of *The Blue Carbuckle* and *The Speckled Band*, both published in 1892.

Paget is also responsible for the deerstalker, first using it on the cover of *The Boscombe Valley Mystery*, published in 1891.

However, Paget never depicted Holmes in both the deerstalker and Inverness at the same time. That was an invention of Hollywood.

What causes sneezing?

Sneezing occurs when the lining of the nose is irritated or swollen. The inside of the nose is crammed with nerve endings. If they are irritated by something inhaled, such as dust or chemicals, the nerves send a message to the nasal and respiratory tissue to go into spasms in an effort to expel the foreign particles. The volume of air expelled during a sneeze is about 500 litres per minute.

A sneeze can also be triggered by other conditions seemingly unrelated to the normal sneeze reflex, including strong emotions and sexual excitement. As well, about one-quarter of the population has the photic sneeze reflex. People with this hereditary condition often sneeze when they look at a bright light. Medical science does not know why this happens.

How much were Judas Iscariot's 30 pieces of silver worth, and what would they be worth today?

The blood money the Romans paid to Judas to betray Jesus could be worth just about anything, depending on how you look at it.

Jerusalem was a cosmopolitan city with many money changers at the time, so there were several types of currency in circulation in the area. Experts do not agree on what monetary system the coins came from, but there are several possibilities.

One coin used in the area at the time was the Greek drachm. A skilled labourer earned about 120 drachma in a year. Collectors today can expect to pay over a hundred dollars for a good example of a drachm. A poor copy not worth a collector's notice is worth about two dollars for its silver content.

The denarius was the silver currency used for dealings with Rome. In the first century AD, a top civil servant might have a salary of 50,000 denarii a year. He could buy a slave boy for 175 denarii, or a litre of wine for 10. A labourer was paid one denarius for a day's work. There is about 11 cents worth of silver in a denarius at today's prices.

The coin most often used for local dealings was the shekel. It was worth four denarii, and contained about 42 cents worth of silver at today's prices. To a collector today, a shekel is worth about $400, although a perfect specimen might fetch $1000.

At the time, the custom of "blood money" dictated that 30 shekels was fair payment for the accidental death of a servant. Some scholars believe the actual cash payment to Judas could have been any amount, and that the "30 pieces of silver" mentioned in St. Matthew's gospel was a cultural reference — a figure of speech.

How do they get the pear into a bottle of Williams Pear Brandy?

Williams pears are grown in Germany, France, Switzerland, and Austria. When the pear trees blossom, brandy bottles are placed over the flowers and are secured to the individual stems. The bottle surrounding the blossom is like a little hothouse, and the pear matures inside the bottle.

When a pear reaches the right size, the stem is cut and the fruit remains in the bottle. The pear is then pricked so it can marinate in the brandy that is poured into the bottle. The entire procedure is labour-intensive, and the end product is very expensive at over $40 a bottle.

Why can ducks stay in the water in winter and not freeze their feet?

Ducks and other shorebirds can overcome cold feet because they are able to regulate the flow of blood in their bodies. When they are in cold water, they send more blood to the arteries in their legs and feet. In addition, these extremities do not require as much heat as the rest of the body, since they are made mostly of bone and tough dead tissue, and very little muscle.

Seals employ a similar mechanism to keep warm. They increase the flow of blood to the extremities in cold weather, and decrease it when it is not required in summer. Seals sunning themselves in summer reduce the blood flow to their flippers and then use them as baffles to radiate excess heat.

The human body has the opposite reaction. Blood in the parts of the body exposed to the cold will retreat to the core of the body. In the case of hypothermia, so much blood has left the extremities that the body goes into shock. In extreme cases, cold blood returning to the heart can cause cardiac arrest.

Why does the letter K signify a strikeout in baseball?

There is more to scorekeeping in baseball than just keeping score. The movements of players around the diamond are noted, as are the actions of the defensive team. The notation on a game's progress looks not unlike the summary of a chess match.

According to the Baseball Hall of Fame, this elaborate system was created by sportswriter Henry Chadwick. Chadwick was an Englishman raised on cricket who moved to the United States and became the premier baseball writer of the 1830s. For a time he was editor of The New York Clipper magazine, the bible for baseball fans of the era.

Chadwick came up with the numbering system for the nine players on the field. 1 is pitcher, 2 is catcher, 3 is first base, and so on. Then there are the abbreviations for the plays: a walk, or base on balls, is "BB"; hit by pitcher is "HBP." It seems simple, but with several plays starting with "S", such as sacrifice bunt and stolen base, it was less confusing to choose another symbol for the strikeout. The "K" for strikeout, instead of coming from the initial letter, is from the final letter of "struck".

After whom was Meech Lake named?

The Meech Lake Accord, the constitutional package introduced by the Mulroney government in 1987 and rejected by the provinces in 1990 after three years of heated debate, put the lake on the map and in the front pages.

Lac Meech, as it is officially known, is named after Asa Meech. He was an American born in 1775 who became a Congregational minister in New England, where he served until 1821. He then moved his family to a lake near the Hull township in the Gatineau hills. Meech was later granted 200 acres of land along the shores of the lake while he continued to preach around Hull and Chelsea. His original house has been extensively restored over the years by the National Capital Commission.

On an 1870 plan used for the restoration, the lake was called Lac Charite. It was said to be the name either for a French settler, Francois Charite, or for an Irishman whose name may have been Lacharity. Asa Meech's name was also on the plan, but it was spelled "Meach."

In 1931, the Geographic Board of Canada approved the name change to Meach Lake. In 1951, Marion Meech, a descendent of As a Meech, asked the Board to change the spelling. The request was turned down because of the spelling on the old plan.

In 1978, the Commission de Toponymie du Quebec changed the name from Meach Lake to Lac Meech.

How did the Conservative and Liberal Parties get their nicknames of Tories and Grits?

The Progressive-Conservative Party gets its nickname from British politics. Tory comes from an Irish word meaning "hunter." The English in 17th century Ireland used tory as a derogatory term for the dispossessed Irish Catholics who became outlaws. The meaning later broadened to include all Irish Royalists and Papists.

Within Britain, supporters of the Catholic King James, the Jacobites, were derisively called Tories. The supporters of the crown formally adopted the name for their party in 1689. The Tory Party changed its name in the 1830s to the Conservative Party because the older name was associated with reaction. When the Conservative Party was formed in Canada, its members were also nicknamed Tories.

The Canadian Liberals are called Grits because of an article in the Toronto Globe in 1849. The Reform Party in Canada West, now Ontario, had liberal views for the time, and one of its members was quoted in the newspaper as saying, "We want men of clear grit." Supporters of the party unofficially dubbed it The Clear Grit Party, and the members were known as Grits.

How do they get the lead into wooden pencils?

Pencils are made of three main ingredients: wood, graphite, and glue. The wood starts out as two flat sheets. Each sheet of wood is one pencil length long, one-half of a pencil diameter deep, and seven pencil diameters wide. The actual dimensions depend on the type of pencil being made.

The sheets are run through a machine that cuts seven parallel grooves into the length of the sheets. A length of pre-cut graphite is then placed into each of the seven grooves of one sheet. Glue is poured into the grooves of the second sheet of wood.

The two sheets of wood are then matched up, with the graphite sandwiched in between. The sandwich is slit lengthwise into seven crude pencils.

The pencils are then shaped and painted. Usually, there is also some lettering stamped into the side of the pencil, and an eraser is attached to one end.

What causes mushrooms in a lawn to form fairy rings?

Fairy rings are the circles of dead grass that appear on a lawn infested with mushrooms. The mushrooms are a part of a fungus called *Marasmius oreades*. The living grass in the middle of the circle is healthy, with the most vigourous growth right along the edge of the fungus. Grass outside the ring is also tallest along the edge of the ring. The fungus kills the grass with which it comes into direct contact, but because the fungus also releases nitrogen, it fertilizes the nearby grass that it is unable to kill.

The mushrooms release spores which, when they germinate, grow out in a radial formation, forming an arc. If there are no barriers, the arc grows into a complete circle. The fungus forms a water-resistant crust in the dead grass, which makes it difficult to kill the infestation with fungicide.

One treatment for fairy ring is the "poke and soak" method. The fungus can be drowned out by first poking deep holes with a potato fork into the crust, and then flooding the ring. The process is repeated until the problem clears up.

What do the letters RRC on the Canadian dollar coin mean?

On the tails side of the loonie, under the bill of the loon, are the letters RRC. They are the initials of the coin's designer, artist Robert Ralph Carmichael.

The design of the new dollar coin intended to replace the paper dollar bill was originally to have been a scaled-down version of the voyageur and Indian found on the existing silver dollar. The dies for this coin were lost in the mail, however, and have never been recovered. After losing the dies, the mint had to find a new design; even if the lost dies were found, they could no longer be used due to the breach of security.

Fortunately, a popular design already existed. Every year, the Canadian mint runs a competition for special coin collections, such as the Olympic coin series. One of the designs submitted in 1977 was of a loon. The entry didn't win, but it was remembered by the judges who were impressed by its uniquely Canadian character. After the voyageur dies disappeared, the loon design was reconsidered.

When the mint expressed renewed interest in his work, Robert Carmichael redesigned his loon. The original design was of an Arctic loon, not the common loon now found on the dollar. The new design was ready in three weeks, and Carmichael received about $5,000 and a great deal of exposure for his efforts.

The new coin was initially met with some resistance, based mostly on a preference for the old paper currency rather than on the design. At first, the coin's nickname, "the loonie", was meant as an insult, but it has since become almost an endearing term for Canada's only commonly circulated coin that is significantly different from its American counterpart.

However, Carmichael is still sensitive to the unofficial name. He prefers to call the one-dollar coin a "loon dollar." Carmichael lives in Echo Bay, near Sault Ste. Marie, where he teaches and continues to produce his art.

Why are the international awards for advertising called the Clio Awards?

The Clio Awards for excellence in advertising in print, radio, and television have been handed out for over 30 years. They are the Oscars of advertising, and the origin of the name is befitting of the advertising industry.

Clio was one of the nine muses of Greek mythology. The muses were the nine daughters of Zeus and the goddess Mnemosyne. Each Muse was identified with an individual art or science. Clio was known as the proclaimer, glorifier, and celebrator of history and accomplishment. She was also the creator of historic and heroic poetry. All important elements of modern advertising.

Why are holes in the ozone not filled in through circulation of the atmosphere?

The circulation of the atmosphere is caused in part by the rotation of the earth. As the earth spins on its axis, the atmosphere is dragged along. As well, circulation is achieved by the wind patterns created by the mix of warm and cool air.

There are two major holes in the ozone layer of the atmosphere. One is the permanent hole over the south pole, and the other is a temporary hole that opens and closes over the north pole. The holes, which are growing as the ozone layer is depleted, are at the poles because the areas closest to the poles do not spin as fast as those closer to the equator in the course of each rotation of the earth. This means the polar atmosphere does not circulate as much as the air over other parts of the planet. There is greater circulation at the north pole than at the south pole because Antarctica is a colder, solid mass whereas the Arctic is part land and part water, and therefore relatively warmer. Consequently, the atmosphere circulates more at the north pole than at the south pole.

Why does spicy food make your tastebuds tingle?

When you eat spicy-hot food, two things occur. First, saliva is produced. Saliva begins the digestive process, breaking down some components of food and providing a liquid medium in which to suspend food particles. When the tastebuds come into contact with the spicy food and saliva mixture, the brain interprets the information received and tells us that the spices are hot.

Secondly, the chemicals that make up the spices react with the pain receptors in the mouth. The receptors respond by numbing the nerves in the mouth. The result is a hot, tingling sensation that can be stimulating or painful, depending on the spice and on the individual.

A drink of water is not always the best solution for a burning mouth. The water mixes with the spicy saliva, spreading the spices even further throughout the mouth before they are finally washed away. Instead, plain bread is usually served with spicy foods as a relief from the hot sensation. As the bread is eaten, it soaks up the spicy saliva, and when swallowed it carries the spice away.

Who invented popcorn?

Popcorn is a delicacy developed by the Indians of North America and dating back thousands of years. Besides eating popped corn, the Indians also used popped corn in head-dresses, necklaces, and in religious ceremonies. According to most sources, a deerskin bag full of popcorn was served at the first Thanksgiving dinner at Plymouth Rock in 1621.

Popcorn's popularity grew during the Depression of the 1930s, when people realized that a little popcorn could go a long way. But its success was clinched when movie theatres across the continent started serving the snack. By 1947, 85 per cent of movie houses were selling popcorn at their concession stands. Today, a movie without popcorn is like Laurel without Hardy.

And those,

Don Anderson, Pat Woods, Ramsay Ross, Steve Halabura, Archie Adams, Brenda Ferster, Lee Hatch, Anne McGee, R.G. Thomas, James Robichaud, Rebbeca Erza, Mike Flattery, Donna Hostyn, Bill Lee, Nadine Thomas, Peggy Bye, Harold McCallum, Derek Lupinksy, Elizabeth Nemis, Kent MacDonald, Carmel Moir, Tony Wyver, Bob Williamson, Cam Bailey, Shirley Martin, Izi Beck, Joy Shabler, Veronica Smedley, Doug Leeds, Barbara Bell, Mrs. Klassen, Peter Anderson, Vye Cyca, Brian Elman, Donald MacWilliams, Cecily Gallant, Sarah Kirkby, Bill White, Alex Grey, Chris Martin, Wendal Jensen, Lloyd Ealy, Moni Minhas, Bob Granger, John Close, Jerry Beaton, Sue Hart, Sandy Kennedy, Raymond Matheson, Monique James, Brian Dodds, Bicks Turney, Bea Fisher, Bruce Thomas, Ragev Ruperel, John Heursink, Marlene Mackie, Bill Pythion, Don Chetner, Martha Baldwin, Martin MacDonald, Ronald Calter, Alan Gibson, Scott Shaw, Leslie Roger, Dale Johnson, Lene Bliek, Marc Benson, Brad Braun, Jack Long, Beverly Mah, David Gilchrist, Roger Hopkins, John Wilks, Daryl Tarasoff, Grant Watson, and Phyllis Erikson,

are the answers to your Good Questions!

If you liked this book, you may want to order the original

That's a Good Question!

How did the TV show "The Fifth Estate" get its name? And what are the other four estates?

What is the oily film on apples from the supermarket?

Why do Bic pens have a hole in the side while other pens don't?

Why are Nova Scotians called "bluenosers"?

Why do men's and women's clothing button on different sides?

Why do most clocks with Roman numerals on the face show the number four as IIII instead of the standard IV?

Are dolphins working for the US Navy?

What were the results of the artificial iceberg experiments of World War II?

What is the origin of the word "ketchup"?

Why is the popcorn at the movies fluffier than home-popped popcorn?

Why are the keys on a typewriter arranged the way they are?

Copies of **That's a Good Question!** are available from the publisher. To order, please complete the order form on the following page.